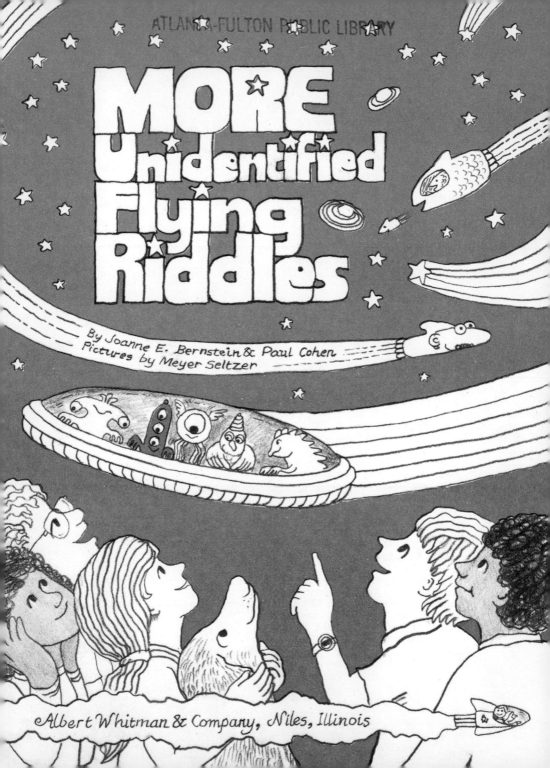

MORE Unidentified Flying Riddles

By Joanne E. Bernstein & Paul Cohen
Pictures by Meyer Seltzer

Albert Whitman & Company, Niles, Illinois

Also by Joanne E. Bernstein and Paul Cohen
Happy Holiday Riddles to You!
Un-Frog-Gettable Riddles
Unidentified Flying Riddles

Library of Congress Cataloging-in-Publication Data

Bernstein, Joanne E.
  More unidentified flying riddles.

  Summary: More than eighty contemporary jokes and
riddles about the sun, moon, stars, astronauts, and
other outer-spatial topics.
    1. Riddles, Juvenile. 2. Outerspace—Juvenile
humor. [1. Outer space—Wit and humor. 2. Riddles.
3. Jokes] I. Cohen, Paul, 1945-   . II. Seltzer,
Meyer, ill. III. Title.
PN6371.5.B397   1985   818'.5402'08   85-15537
ISBN 0-8075-5279-8 (lib. bdg.)

Illustrations © 1985 by Meyer Seltzer
Text © 1985 by Joanne Bernstein and Paul Cohen
Published in 1985 by Albert Whitman & Company, Niles, Illinois
Published simultaneously in Canada
by General Publishing, Limited, Toronto
All rights reserved. Printed in U.S.A.
10   9   8   7   6   5   4   3   2

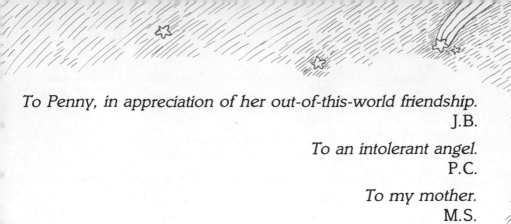

To Penny, in appreciation of her out-of-this-world friendship.
J.B.

To an intolerant angel.
P.C.

To my mother.
M.S.

Don't Look Down!

What kind of music do astronauts dance to on the moon?
Moon rock.

Which relative visited the astronauts in space?
Auntie Gravity.

Why can't you understand astronauts' jokes?
They're over your head.

What does an astronaut do in the morning before he gets dressed?
He takes a meteor shower.

Why do astronauts worry about their jobs?
Every time they're sent into space, they're fired.

Why do astronauts go to the doctor before they're launched into space?
They have to get their booster shots.

Reporter to astronaut: What is the secret of space travel?
Astronaut: Don't look down.

What do astronauts argue about?
Who gets to sit by the window.

First astronaut: We're going faster than the speed of sound.
Second astronaut: What?

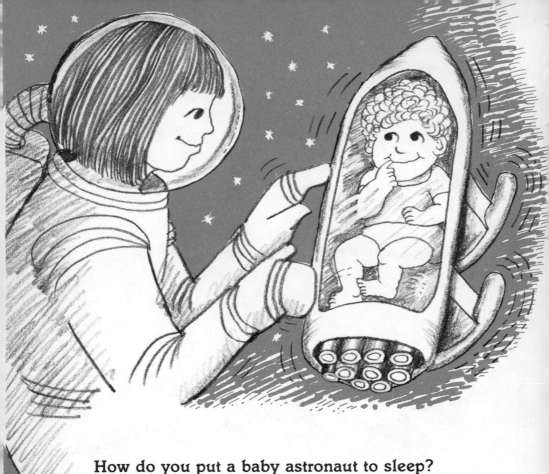

How do you put a baby astronaut to sleep?
You rock-et.

What did the astronaut say when the rocket electricity system broke down?
"AC come, AC go."

Why couldn't the astronaut make cinnamon toast?
He was outer spice.

How do you make an astronaut sandwich?
With a lot of launch meat.

How is an astronaut like a football player?
They both make touchdowns.

How does ground control talk with astronauts in space?
By long distance.

How do astronauts tell time?
They use a sundial.

How do astronauts get across the moon's seas?
They use row-bots.

What do astronauts do when they get thirsty?
Take a drink from the Big Dipper.

Who made a spaceship that couldn't get off the ground?
The Wrong Brothers.

What cleans Saturn's rings from the bathtub?
Halley's Comet.

What do people say when they see Halley's comet return every seventy-six years?
"Halley-lujah!"

Who came back from space in a coonskin cap?
Davy Rockett.

Does St. Nick travel over Russian rooftops on Christmas Eve?
No, but Sputnik does.

Who was the first nuclear scientist?
Eve, because she knew all about the atom (Adam).

What is an atom?
A guy who went around with Eve.

What did Luke Skywalker say after losing his best friend?
"Look, Ma, no Han."

How did Mary's little lamb go to Mars?
By rocket sheep.

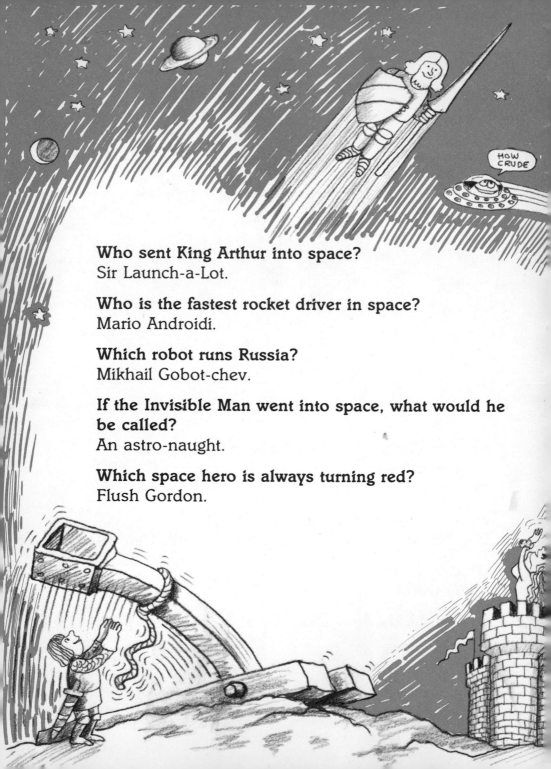

Who sent King Arthur into space?
Sir Launch-a-Lot.

Who is the fastest rocket driver in space?
Mario Androidi.

Which robot runs Russia?
Mikhail Gobot-chev.

If the Invisible Man went into space, what would he be called?
An astro-naught.

Which space hero is always turning red?
Flush Gordon.

HOW
CRUDE

Martian Along

What did the Martian say when his spaceship landed at the North Pole?
"Take me to your heater."

What did the Martian say when he landed in the flower bed?
"Take me to your weeder."

First Martian: Which is more important, the sun or the moon?
Second Martian: The moon. It shines when it is dark, but the sun shines when it is light anyway.

Which aliens are like soldiers?
Martians, because they go Martian along.

Two Martians landed next to a traffic light. "I saw her first," one said.

"So what," the other replied. "I'm the one she winked at."

What did the Martian say to the radar antenna? "If you keep turning your head around like that, it's going to fall off."

What did the Martian's mother say when he returned from an invasion? "Where on Earth have you been?"

What can Martians have that no one else can have?
Baby Martians.

Why did the Martian child want to go to Saturn?
He couldn't wait to play with the hula hoops.

Why did the Martian take a shovel into space?
To dig a black hole.

What do Martians put in their cocoa?
Martian-mallows.

Blast Off!

How many sides does a spaceship have?
Two—the inside and the outside.

What's as big as a rocket yet weighs nothing?
A rocket's shadow.

How many feet are there in a spaceship?
Twice as many as there are people.

What goes up when you count down?
A spaceship.

How could you knock a tennis ball into orbit?
With a tennis rocket.

Which spaceship was always making excuses?
Apollo G.

Why is it easy to get a spaceship back to Earth?
It's downhill all the way.

What kinds of trips does the new rabbit rocket make?
Only short hops.

Moonkind

ONE GIANT STEP FOR MOONKIND

Who was the first man in space?
The man in the moon.

Would we survive if the left side of the moon disappeared?
Yes, because then it would be all right.

What do they drink on the moon?
Craterade.

How many balls of string would it take to reach the moon?
Only one if it were long enough.

Joe: I hear the moon is going broke.
Steve: What makes you think that?
Joe: Well, it said in the paper that the moon was down to its last quarter.

What's the newest form of lunar transport?
The moon-o-rail.

What kind of dog can live on the moon?
The Mexican 'airless (hairless).

Why is a half moon heavier than a full moon?
Because a full moon is lighter.

Teacher: Which is farther away, South America or the moon?
Student: South America.
Teacher: What makes you think that?
Student: We can see the moon, but we can't see South America.

How does the Man in the Moon cut his hair?
'Eclipse it. (He clips it.)

What travels around the earth without using a single drop of fuel?
The moon.

Why would they want the letters *HIJKLMNO* on the moon?
It's the formula for water—H_2O (*H* to *O*).

Why is it all right to go to crowded restaurants on the moon?
There's only one sixth of the wait (weight).

Sunny Business

What happens when the sun gets tired?
It sets a while.

Why is a cat like the sun?
Both go out at night.

What color would you paint the sun and the wind?
The sun rose and the wind blue (blew).

What's the difference between the sun and a loaf of bread?
One rises from the east, the other from the yeast.

What will happen when the sun shines at night?
That'll be the day.

Who was the first settler in the American West?
The sun.

Planet of the Oops

What planet is round, purple, and orbits the sun?
The Planet of the Grapes.

What planet is famous for its bananas?
The Planet of the Apes.

How do you get our planet to go backwards?
Put it in revearth.

Older sister: That planet over there is Mars.
Younger sister: Then that other must be Pa's.

On what planet are the people always falling on their faces?
The Planet of the Oops.

And how do they get there?
They just take a little trip.

What planet can you see every day?
Earth.

How do we know there are telephones on Saturn?
Because of all the rings.

The All-Star Game

What vegetable do you eat in space?
Capri-corn.

Who's Irish and lives in the sky?
O'Ryan the Hunter.

What's the naked constellation?
The Great Bare.

What is a waiter's least favorite constellation?
The Crab.

What's a waiter's favorite constellation?
The Big Tipper.

What do the losers in the Ms. Universe contest get?
Constellation prizes.

What would you call a fight between Taurus the Bull and the cow that jumped over the moon?
Steer Wars.

Pete: Stars have funny names.
Sue: What do you mean?
Pete: Well, there's one called the Dog Star.
Sue: Are you Sirius?

Why does a movie fan like to visit the planetarium?
It's always an all-star show.

What constellations are used to make ice-cream cones?
The Big and Little Dippers.

How are false teeth like stars?
They come out at night.

Data's Right!

What's a robot's favorite kind of music?
Heavy metal.

What killed the robot's computer?
A terminal illness.

How do you compliment a Go-Bot?
You say, "Data boy!"

How does a transformer shave?
With a laser razor.

What do you say when a robot dies?
"Gear today, gone tomorrow."

What does it say on robot tombstones?
"Rust in peace."

What does an outer-space frog say?
"Robot, robot."

Spaced Out

GOOD MORNING!
THIS IS LIGHT, COMING TO YOU COURTESY OF THE SUN AT 186,000 MILES PER SECOND.

GRMPHH

How fast does light travel?
I'm not sure, but it gets here too early in the morning.

What do you call a drooling satellite?
Spit-nik.

Why can't satellites make much progress?
They keep going around in circles.

What's the best way to see flying saucers?
Tickle a waiter.

Why do dogs prefer food from outer space?
It's meteor.

How do you catch an insect in outer space?
With a Venus flytrap.

What is a satellite?
What you put on your horse if you're going to ride after dark.

What's the difference between a meteorite and fog?
One hit the earth, the other mist.

What surprising things happen every twenty-four hours?
Day breaks but doesn't fall; night falls but doesn't break.

How is an astronomer like an evening security guard?
They're both night watchmen.

Vat do you call a rotating calf in space?
A spinning veal.

What missile sneaks up on you?
The Nike.

Where do aliens go fishing?
In the galax-seas.

When do space children go to school?
From Moonday to Saturnday.

When does the astro-child get a good report at the dentist's?
When the dentist says, "No gravities!"

What beam weighs the least?
A light beam.

What kinds of blooms would you bring back from space?
Sun flowers.

What kind of sentence would you get if you broke the law of gravity?
A suspended one.

Why are there no public parking garages in space?
There are enough meteors (meters) to go around.

Which studio makes all the outer space movies?
Universal.

How does an astronaut say goodbye?
3-2-1- blast off!

This book is the second intergalactic collaboration for **Joanne Bernstein** and **Paul Cohen**. The astronomical success of their first effort, *Unidentified Flying Riddles*, demanded an encore, and they were more than sequel to the task.

Meyer Seltzer has been drawing and reading about space subjects since he was a young boy. Even now, many people think that he is a space cadet.

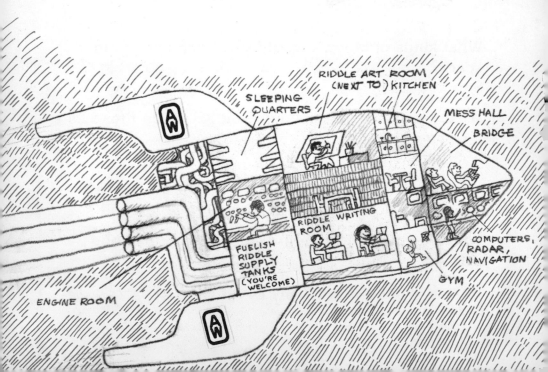

J

398.8   Bernstein, Joanne E.
BERNSTEI
N
     More unidentified flying riddles /
-- Niles, Ill. : A. Whitman, 1985.
     [32] p. : ill. (some col.) ; 22 cm.
     Sequel to: Unidentified flying
riddles.
     Summary More than eighty
contemporary jokes and riddles about
the sun, moon, stars, astronauts, and
other outer-spatial topics. 85015537
/AC/r86

05/26/87   0619624
                         Card 1 of 2